CREATIVE LIVES

Coco Chanel

JEREMY WALLIS

Heinemann Library
Chicago, Illinois

© 2002 Reed Educational & Professional Publishing
Published by Heinemann Library,
an imprint of Reed Educational & Professional Publishing,
Chicago, Illinois

Customer Service 888-454-2279
Visit our website at www.heinemannlibrary.com

Designed by Tinstar
Originated by Ambassador Litho
Printed and bound in Hong Kong/China

06 05 04 03 02
10 9 8 7 6 5 4 3 2 1

Library of Congress Cataloging-in-Publication Data
Wallis, Jeremy.
  Coco Chanel / By Jeremy Wallis.
    p. cm. -- (Creative lives)
Includes bibliographical references and index.
  ISBN 1-58810-202-5
  1. Chanel, Coco, 1883-1971--Juvenile literature. 2. Women fashion designers--France--Biography--Juvenile literature. 3. Costume design--France--History--20th century--Juvenile literature. [1. Chanel, Coco, 1883-1971. 2. Fashion designers. 3. Women--Biography.] I. Title. II. Series.
  TT505.C45 W35 2001
  746.9'2'092--dc21

Acknowledgments
The author and publishers are grateful to the following for permission to reproduce copyright material:
p. 4, Cecil Beaton/Sotheby's London; pp. 5, 19, 25, Condé Nast Publications Inc; pp. 6, 29, 31, Hulton Getty; p. 8, Harlingue-Viollet; pp. 10, 36, 53, AKG; p. 11, Hutin, Compiégne; pp. 12, 15, 49, Rue des Archives; p. 13, Bibliotheque Nationale; p. 16, Sygma; p. 17, Lebrecht Collection; p. 21, Roger Schall; p. 23, Musée des Arts Décoratifs, Paris; pp. 24, 32, 47, 35, House of Chanel, France; p. 26, Bettmann/Corbis; p. 28, Wladimir Rehbinder, courtesy of Vogue, Paris; pp. 30, 33, 51, Topham; p. 34, John Miehle/Kobal; pp. 37, 44, Roger Viollet; p. 38, P. Horst/Vogue; p. 39, John Rawlings/Vogue; p. 40, F. Kollar/Ministére de la Culture, Paris; p. 41, Corbis; p. 48, Robert Doisneau/Rapho/Network; p. 54, Horst.

Cover photograph reproduced with permission of Corbis.

Every effort has been made to contact copyright holders of any material reproduced in this book. Any omissions will be rectified in subsequent printings if notice is given to the publisher.

Some words are shown in bold, **like this.** You can find out what they mean by looking in the glossary.

Contents

Introduction

" In 1971, André Malraux, writer and French Minister of Culture, said: *"From this century, in France, three names will remain: De Gaulle, Picasso, and Chanel."* "

You may only know the name *Chanel* from the label on a perfume bottle. But the story of Gabrielle "Coco" Chanel is of interest to anyone curious about fashion, art, and history in the twentieth century. Chanel was a designer, but she was also involved in theater, ballet, and the movies, and she lived through major events in world history, such as World War I, the **Great Depression,** and World War II.

For many, Chanel epitomizes the **Jazz Age**—a glamorous world of beautiful people living in luxury between the two world wars, before **depression,** war, and hunger swept the globe.

It would be wrong to dismiss Chanel simply as a dressmaker who made herself rich and famous by dressing wealthy clients. In fact, she was one of the most remarkable women of the century, living at a time of great artistic, political, and social change. Chanel changed the way that women dressed at the same time as people were starting to demand **women's rights** and a **mass market** for women's fashion was developing. If the changes in women's

In this photograph by Cecil Beaton, Gabrielle "Coco" Chanel strikes a pose in evening dress, between two Nubian statues.

status between 1918 and the 1970s can be called a **revolution,** then it can be said that Chanel designed the uniforms for that revolution.

Chanel began designing clothes at a time when women's bodies were constrained by whalebone corsets and complicated trimmings and accessories—when they had to wear uncomfortable outfits that even lacked pockets. Of the elaborate hats that were popular when she was a young designer, Chanel once asked, "How can a brain work under those things?"

Function versus form

Chanel changed women's clothes to reflect their lives. She let function determine form, so that the purpose of a costume influenced its design. Her outfits were comfortable, sensible, stylish, and, for many people, affordable. She was also never afraid to criticize designers who failed to recognize the real shape of women's bodies: "Someone tells you: 'The shoulder is on the back.' I've never seen women with shoulders on their backs."

For years, Chanel's influence on women's fashion was total. She was the first designer to dress women in pants, she popularized short hair, and she revolutionized swim and sportswear. As a fashion innovator, anything she did was noticed. One story tells of Chanel standing on the deck of a yacht. Feeling cold, she borrowed a man's jacket, but because the sleeves were too long she draped it over her shoulders—and accidentally started a fashion copied by thousands. Coco is even credited with making suntans fashionable.

This illustration of Chanel's jersey clothing was printed in *Vogue* in 1928.

This photo of Chanel in a straw cloche hat was taken in 1929.

Chanel was also an innovative businesswoman. Her simple garments could be reproduced easily by seamstresses or department stores. The fashion magazine *Vogue* compared her most famous design—the "little black dress"—to the Ford Model-T car, saying it was practical, stylish, and sure to be imitated. She launched Chanel No.5, the first perfume to bear a designer's name, and recognized that perfume, not **haute couture,** was the secret of financial success. Her expensive clothes sold Chanel style, but Chanel No.5 was the essence of elegance that any woman could afford.

Chanel was friends with the artists of the **avant-garde.** She borrowed ideas from wherever she saw fit, and was influenced by paintings, music, theater, and the ballet. Chanel was inspired by Egyptian artifacts, Russian peasant and gypsy styles, men's clothing, sportswear, and Asian clothing.

Chanel's life was influenced by the events of the twentieth century; from World War I, the roaring twenties, the Wall Street Crash and the **Great Depression** to World War II, the New Look of the 1950s, and the alternative culture of the 1960s. When she died in 1971, she controlled a **multinational** fashion empire—quite an achievement for a child born in poverty and brought up in an orphanage.

The Beginnings

Who was Coco Chanel? It is hard to say, because Chanel told stories about herself and her past. Even when she was old, and had spent many decades in the limelight, she told the story of her life the way she wanted it remembered. Coco Chanel created more than clothes, hats, and jewelry; she invented herself.

Born Gabrielle Chanel, she was the second child of a traveling salesman. Her father, Albert Chanel, moved from town to town selling buttons, hats, and kitchen aprons at the town markets. Her mother was Jeanne Devolle. Albert met Jeanne in 1881, when she was seventeen years old and still living with her family in the village of Courpière in France. In January 1882 he left, leaving Jeanne pregnant. Jeanne discovered where Albert was and, alone and heavily pregnant, she traveled 124 miles (200 kilometers) to a village called Aubenas, where Albert was renting a room in a tavern. The couple's first daughter, Julia, was born there in September 1882. Three months later, after she and Albert moved to Saumur, Jeanne became pregnant again.

Gabrielle was born in the Saumur **hospice** on August 19, 1883. Hospice staff gave her the name Gabrielle, and she would always resent it. When two **illiterate** hospice employees registered her birth at the town hall, they took no documents to confirm the status of parents or child. The deputy mayor improvised, misspelling her last name "Chasnel" on the birth certificate.

Chanel ignored the mistake; to correct it might have revealed her hospice birth. Although her parents married after she was born, Gabrielle always feared people might learn of her **illegitimacy.** In later life, she claimed that her father had been a wealthy horse trader. She paid her siblings to keep quiet about her past, and even denied their existence. To some, Gabrielle explained the manner of her birth as an accident that befell her mother while traveling to join her husband. To others, she claimed she had been born on a train.

After Gabrielle, Jeanne gave birth in quick succession to Alphonse, Antoinette, and Lucien. A third son died in infancy. The children often

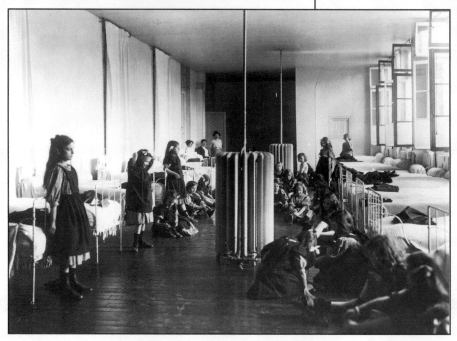

Life in an orphanage in France at the end of the nineteenth century was disciplined and orderly. Chanel benefitted from this strict environment.

stayed with Jeanne's family in Courpière. Life on the road, poverty, and constant pregnancies destroyed Jeanne's health, and she fell ill. In 1895, when Gabrielle was 12 years old, Jeanne was found dead in her room. She was only 32 years old. Albert Chanel, who was away at the time, abandoned his children and disappeared.

Members of Jeanne's family were happy to have the children at holiday time, but could not take them in permanently. Instead, Julia, Gabrielle, and Antoinette spent six years in an orphanage run by sisters of the Congregation of the Sacred Heart of Mary at Aubazine. Alphonse and baby Lucien were sent to live and work on a farm.

> " Chanel found strength in suffering. She once said, *"I've been ungrateful toward the odious aunts [but] I owe them everything. A child in revolt becomes a person with armor and strength … It's the mean and nasty aunts who create winners, and give them **inferiority complexes** … Under nastiness looms strength."* "

As an adult, Chanel sliced years off her age and dropped Julia, Alphonse, and Lucien from her life story. She told people she was six when her mother died and rarely talked of the orphanage, describing the nuns as "aunts."

Life in the orphanage was hard, but Gabrielle took pleasure in the cleanliness, simplicity, and orderliness at Aubazine. She described herself as fierce, pretty, and restless. She also knew she was different: "I was a pest, a thief, someone who listens at doors. Today, like back then, arrogance is in everything I do." She found comfort in being alone, and spent time in cemeteries talking to the dead. To avoid embarrassment about her family background, Gabrielle told her classmates that her father was seeking his fortune in America and would come back for her when he was rich. In reality, she never saw him again.

During the holidays with her grandparents, Gabrielle grew close to Adrienne, an aunt her age. They often passed themselves off as sisters. Adrienne's older sister, Louise, rescued Gabrielle's brothers from the farm and put them into apprenticeships with salesmen. Gabrielle had been taught to sew at the orphanage, but Louise showed her how to sew with imagination.

After six years at the orphanage, Julia and Gabrielle attended boarding school in Moulins, a small **garrison town.** Antoinette joined them a year later. The girls relied on charity to pay for lodging and food, and worked to pay their school fees. To cater to the military, Moulins had many restaurants, cafés, and tailors' shops. By the age of twenty, Gabrielle had a reputation as a skilled dressmaker. She also worked with Adrienne in a tailor's shop to supplement her income. Soon young cavalry officers were coming into the shop as much to see "The Three Graces"—as Gabrielle, Adrienne, and the sixteen-year-old Antoinette were nicknamed—as they were to have their uniforms altered.

The most fashionable entertainment of the day was the *café concert*. There were many in Moulins, well attended by young officers and their families. Gabrielle worked hard as a dressmaker and tailor's assistant, but she had serious ambitions to become a singer and entertainer.

The girls started to accept invitations to concerts at a large, popular café called La Rotonde. In the days before microphones, singers needed to take regular breaks to rest their voices. Young women sat on stage and filled in during these pauses. Audiences pelted these young substitutes with trash if their performances were not satisfactory.

This picture of Chanel was taken around 1909, at the time when she was a regular singer at La Rotonde.

Gabrielle took a turn at singing. Her voice was not strong, but she gave a popular performance with a song about a young woman looking for her dog. "I've lost my poor Coco," she sang, "Coco my lovable dog." Chanel became a regular. Audiences knew her as *La Petite* Coco, meaning "Little Coco," and the name stuck. Chanel eventually accepted the fact that she had limited abilities as a singer and that she would never have career as a *café concert* performer, but her love of the stage would often emerge in later life.

Moving On

When she was 21 years old, Chanel became involved with Etienne Balsan, an army officer three years older than she was. Etienne was the wayward son of a rich family. His passion was horses: Once he got out of the army, he wanted to breed racehorses.

Some biographers believe that Chanel became pregnant by Etienne early in their relationship. Soon after, Julia, Chanel's sister, also became pregnant. Chanel had no intention of bringing up an **illegitimate** child, as her sister was about to do, and some biographers think that she had a surgery to avoid having the child. The surgery may have left her unable to have children in later life.

In 1905 Etienne left the army and asked Chanel to visit his home, Royallieu. Coco realized that she would never have a singing career, and she lacked the **dowry** needed to marry a respectable young man. She accepted Etienne's invitation. She would stay at Royallieu for years.

This is a photo of Royallieu, where Coco lived with Etienne and the Balsan family for three years.

Life at Royallieu

Like many rich young men, Etienne Balsan was indulged by his family. He surrounded himself with famous and wealthy people. His acquaintances—aristocrats, sportsmen, racehorse owners—liked to bring women who were not their wives to Royallieu. Many of these female guests were themselves unconventional and independent—women like Gabrielle Dorziat, a well-known actress of the time who became a close friend of Chanel's.

Chanel spent her years at Royallieu learning to ride horses, attending horse races and parties, and enjoying the luxuries of the **belle époque.** She had a role that was common at the time: She was a woman who lived as a wealthy man's wife but whom, because she was neither respectable nor aristocratic enough, he could not marry.

Many women lived the way that Chanel did. The most famous of these women were the "diamond crunchers," so-called because they received valuable love tokens such as diamonds. But a new group of women was emerging—the **Claudines.** Inspired by the women in the popular novels of a French author named Colette, *Claudines* were young, quick-witted, stylish, defiant, and ready to break social restrictions. This "new woman" was celebrated in plays, paintings, and songs. The campaign for women's **suffrage** was intense at this time. Women were becoming better educated and were

The men and women in this busy tavern in France during the *belle époque*, around 1900, model the fashions of the time.

This fashion photograph by Seeberger Frères, from around 1909, shows the fussy hats and clothes of the period.

soon allowed to enter professions such as the law. Like a typical *Claudine*, Chanel set herself apart from other women by the way she dressed and the way she lived. She was unmarried, and from a poor family, so she was not a society woman, but she was not a diamond cruncher either.

Chanel's first fashions

In contrast to the fashions worn by other women, Chanel preferred plain clothes. She later confessed that when she arrived at Royallieu, her wardrobe consisted of two tailored suits and a jacket, adding that the origins of her outfits were the tailored clothes she had worn as a teenager.

When riding, a skill that earned her the admiration of Etienne and his friends, Chanel was every inch the modern sportswoman. She straddled the horse rather than riding sidesaddle, and she raided Etienne's wardrobe for clothes ideas. She designed her own outfits: riding breeches cut from a stable-groom's pattern, a riding-jacket, and a shirt with a collar and tie. This was **radical** at a time when most women rode sidesaddle and wore safety skirts over their breeches.

Chanel still suffered from an **inferiority complex.** Intimidated by the beauty and status of the women guests at Royallieu, and undermined by her lowly social status, Chanel compensated with a sarcastic manner and wit. Yet all the while, she carefully observed the behavior and **etiquette** of the social **elite** she and Etienne entertained.

Etienne and Coco got along well, but she later confessed she did not love him. Etienne's family thought he would never make a name for himself, and one account says that Etienne's brother actually asked Chanel to marry Etienne and make him "respectable." Chanel turned the offer down.

Life at Royallieu was easy. Removed from the outside world, the pattern of Chanel's life was straightforward. Friends and acquaintances recalled how she would often emerge from her room only at lunchtime, unless a horse ride was promised, in which case she would be dressed and eager to go out at the break of dawn.

Chanel grew bored. To keep herself occupied, she bought plain straw hats at the Galeries Lafayette store in Paris and decorated and trimmed them herself. These were much more attractive than the fussy plumed hats of the time, and women friends often asked where she bought them. Emilienne d'Alençon, an infamous diamond cruncher and one of Etienne's former girlfriends, brought Chanel to wider public attention by wearing a hat Chanel had designed to a horse race. Coco was encouraged by the popularity of her hats, and asked Etienne to finance a hat store in Paris.

France and the *belle époque*

The *belle époque*—a period in France that lasted from 1900 until the beginning of World War I—was a prosperous time and also a time of exciting change.

Industrialization increased the population in the cities, and created new social problems. Working people campaigned to improve their lives. Leisure time—picnics, horse races, boating trips—became important as people took breaks from city life, encouraged by the development of the railways. The French government became **nationalistic**, anti-**socialist**, and anti-German, fearful of socialist **revolution** and German aggression. In the arts, France was recognized as the center of **Modernism**.

New Influences
and Directions

In 1908, while Etienne thought about Chanel's business idea, they traveled to hunt in the Pyrenees. On the trails below the snow-capped mountains, Chanel met the love of her life: Arthur Capel, an Englishman everyone called "Boy."

Boy Capel had financial interests in coal and shipping and was an excellent horseman. He and Coco spent hours in each other's company. When Coco learned one evening that Boy was leaving for Paris, she wrote a note to Etienne: "I am leaving with Boy. Forgive me, but I love him."

She left without even a suitcase. Chanel later told people she was an awkward eighteen-year-old when she met Boy. In fact, she was 25. Coco moved into Boy's apartment in Paris. Many people in polite society frowned upon their relationship because they were not married, but Boy introduced Coco to a new circle of painters, writers, and actors who were not upset by their unconventional relationship.

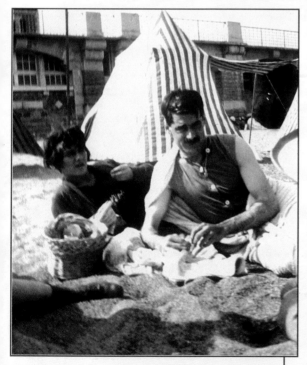

Coco and Boy enjoyed going to the beach.

The beginnings of the Chanel empire

Chanel remained on good terms with Etienne. Though he refused to finance her hat store, he agreed to let her use his apartment in Paris as a base. The business opened in 1909.

Soon, many of Chanel's female acquaintances were buying her stylish hats. They, in turn, introduced them to their friends. Although Chanel worked hard, she was soon forced to employ a professional **milliner** and, later, two assistants. Recognizing her abilities and her ambition, Boy loaned Chanel money to open a clothing store. The store, Chanel Modes, opened in 1910.

Chanel the brand

Chanel recognized the importance of the relationship between the worlds of theater and fashion. In the days before television, movies, and radio, stage actresses and dancers established fashion trends that were featured in newspapers and fashion magazines.

In 1910, actress Lucienne Roger wore a Chanel hat on the cover of a magazine. There were enthusiastic reviews, and illustrations of other actresses wearing Chanel hats. Soon Gabrielle Dorziat was buying all her hats from Chanel Modes; she wore Chanel hats on stage and was photographed wearing one in a fashion magazine in 1912.

Chanel's name became as well known as the stars for whom she worked. But, unlike them, she liked to preserve an air of mystery and often hid in the back room of the store, out of sight. "A client seen is a client lost," she once said.

By 1913, Chanel's business was financially secure. When her older sister, Julia, died suddenly, Coco was able to assume financial responsibility for the education of Julia's son, André Palasse. She also employed her younger sister, Antoinette, who no longer had Julia to rely on.

Gabrielle Dorziat, a famous actress, was photographed wearing a Chanel hat in 1912.

The fashion houses of Paris

In Paris in the first decades of the twentieth century, there were several established fashion houses—such as Worth, Doucet, and Paquin—and a publishing industry that thrived on reporting what society figures and actresses were wearing. Fashion magazines carried news of the latest styles: rigid corsets that pinched the waist so tightly they made eating difficult and affected breathing; layers of skirts; trimmings of lace, beads, sequins, and feathers. Then, as now, popular culture had a major influence on fashion. For example, in 1908, Paul Poiret introduced a new, looser style inspired by Eastern fashion and Serge Diaghilev's modern ballet company, the Ballets Russes.

Moving in unfamiliar circles

Chanel's interest in the arts grew. Seeing the talented modern dancer Isadora Duncan perform inspired Chanel to take dance lessons. Her teacher, a former performer named Caryathis, was blunt: Coco had no talent. However, she invited Chanel to the opening night of *The Rite of Spring,* a ballet by Igor Stravinsky, performed by the Ballets Russes.

The Ballets Russes production of *The Rite of Spring* caused riots in the theater. Chanel secretly funded a revival of this ballet, and had a relationship with Stravinsky, the composer.

17

A previous Stravinsky ballet, *The Firebird*, had been a sensation, and Parisians looked forward to the new piece. It opened on May 13, 1913. Despite its title, *The Rite of Spring* is not full of love and spring flowers; it is a powerful representation in music and dance of a **pagan fertility rite.** At the most dramatic moment, a young woman is killed to please the gods because they made the soil fertile. The music and the story were unlike anything the audience had seen before. Chanel was at the opening night, and watched in amazement as the audience rioted. The dancers were booed, and Stravinsky took refuge backstage while his opponents and supporters fought in the aisles. Attending the opening night was the start of Chanel's association with the **avant-garde,** and with Diaghilev and Stravinsky in particular.

Deauville

In the summer of 1913, Boy Capel rented a suite at the grand Hotel Normandy in Deauville. Every summer, wealthy visitors filled this beach resort. They entertained themselves by sailing, gambling, and watching horse races. Capel realized Deauville was a perfect market for Chanel. She soon left Antoinette in charge of Chanel Modes in Paris and opened a shop on the most stylish street in Deauville.

Until 1913, the ocean was for looking at or sailing on. Only a few people, including Chanel, actually swam in it. The rich sneered at suntans as the mark of a peasant lifestyle spent working outside in the sun. Instead, the wealthy protected their fair complexions with **parasols** and hats. However, sports and outdoor activities were becoming both popular and fashionable. Coco conquered Deauville by introducing a fashion that fit the new outdoor trend—sportswear.

Chanel liked the sweaters worn by English sailors. She picked one up at a polo match because she was cold. It was too big, so she cut the front open so it would not have to be pulled over the head, and added ribbons and a knotted belt. "People asked me, 'Where did you find that dress?' I said, 'If you like it I'll sell it to you.' I sold ten like that … My fortune is built on that old jersey I put on because I was cold."

In creating this new design from an old sweater, Chanel wrote the rules that marked her career as a designer: function dictated form. By 1917, the loose, comfortable sailor sweater was immensely popular around the world.

This illustration of a model wearing the fashionable Chanel sailor sweater was printed in *Vogue* in June, 1917.

Chanel had a champion in the cartoonist Sem, who drew cartoons comparing her simple, straightforward designs to the overly-fussy fashions of the time. He also showed Chanel as a society personality who was changing the social standing of designers. Before Chanel, fashion designers were considered tradespeople. Their clients would never have expected to see them in a social situation. Chanel had friends who were avant-garde artists, musicians, and actors, and she attended society functions such as opening nights at the theater and ballet. Soon, designers were the people to be seen with. "I started a fashion," Chanel said, "**couturiers** as stars."

Fame and Fortune
during World War I

During World War I, away from the fighting, there were winners as well as losers. Boy Capel's interests in coal and shipping and his contacts in the British and French governments made him wealthy and influential. Coco also emerged a winner. Because of **rationing** and the seriousness of the war, simplicity became fashionable. Fashion was turned upside down. As women became involved in the war effort, clothing had to suit their active lifestyle.

When war was declared, most people vacationing in Deauville went home. Boy returned to England. As the German army advanced on Paris, panic gripped the city. Theaters, stores, and galleries were closed. The French government moved to Bordeaux, and resources were diverted to prepare defenses for Paris. Deauville now filled with wealthy women, who were sent away from the capital by their husbands. Shrewdly, Chanel kept her store open—it was the only one left in town. Antoinette and Adrienne left the Paris store and joined her once more.

Modesty prevails

There was a new demand for simple, yet flattering, fashion. Excessive displays were considered bad taste when young men were dying on the front lines. By the end of 1914, Paris was no longer threatened by the Germans. As the military situation stabilized, stores reopened and business resumed.

The government allowed theaters to reopen, but banned jewelry and evening dress. Chanel's style was perfect: Her smart, functional look suited the new mood in fashion. Women were encouraged to lose weight to use less fabric. Coco sold the new slimness: "with the [war] ... all my clients lost weight, to 'become skinny like Coco'." Coco cut her hair short—in the "bobbed" style—and blamed her new look, in the Chanel legend, on an accident with a broken water heater. The short, easy-to-care-for cut was stylish and practical. Women loved it.

In 1915, Chanel opened a boutique in Biarritz, a resort town close to Spain. Biarritz attracted visitors from Spain, where elegance was still in fashion. Spanish and American women soon formed a large part of Chanel's clientele. *Harper's Bazaar* magazine announced, "The woman who hasn't at least one Chanel is hopelessly out of the running in fashion." By 1916, about 300 people were employed by Chanel in Paris, Deauville, and Biarritz.

The Chanel method

In Biarritz, Chanel's fashion house sold made-to-order outfits to wealthy Parisians living out the war in **exile.** Sixty people were employed in the shop and workrooms. Despite the war, there was still a trade in luxury fabrics: Chanel established relationships with weaving factories and dyers in France, England, and Scotland.

Many of Chanel's favorite models and mannequins looked like Coco herself. She is shown here with a group of mannequins in the 1930s.

Chanel liked people to think she was a lady of leisure. But she actually worked very hard—sometimes for up to seven hours on a single outfit. She did not sketch outfits but created them by draping material around young women, called **mannequins,** who were paid to stand still for a long time. She crouched before them, tugging, stretching, folding, and stitching, with her scissors dangling from a ribbon around her neck.

The jersey revolution

Knitted jersey material was introduced around 1880. Made of finely knitted wool, jersey clung to the body and stretched into shape. It was used to make men's underwear and sportswear. In 1916, Jean Rodier, a fabric manufacturer, offered Chanel a huge stock of jersey. The natural stretch made it difficult to sew, but Chanel solved the problem by making simple shapes. Many people were shocked that Chanel was using this material for women's clothes, but with these garments, she turned knitted jersey into high fashion. In 1917, *Vogue* called the House of Chanel "the Jersey House." A fashionable Paris magazine featured Chanel's jersey designs in March 1917.

First, a blueprint was made in cheap muslin fabric. When it was perfect—and up to 30 might be created before Chanel thought it was—the muslin was used as a pattern to make the final garment in the selected fabric.

Any **mannequin** who complained or moved while posing would be jabbed by Chanel's pins. The mannequins were not well paid. Chanel said, "They're beautiful. Let them take lovers."

Waking up famous

By the end of the war, in November 1918, 1.5 million Frenchmen had been killed, and the treasury had been emptied. The country was in ruins. Old beliefs and ways of life disappeared. There were irreversible changes in culture and in the way women saw their place in the world.

Paris quickly recovered in the post-war years and soon dominated art, culture, fashion, and design. The poet Gertrude Stein said Paris was "where the twentieth century is." It was a city where you could do or get anything, where the sounds of dancing and jazz were heard all night long.

Praised along with the **avant-garde** artist Pablo Picasso and the writer Jean Cocteau, everything was going right for Coco. "1919 was the year I woke up famous,"she said. But tragedy loomed.

These Chanel jersey outfits were illustrated in a French fashion magazine in 1917. Chanel used a fabric used by swimmers, bicycle riders, and fishermen to create fashion.

Deaths and depression

Chanel and Boy had seen great success, but a distance had grown between them. In 1918, Boy had married Lady Diana Wyndham. In spite of his marriage, he still wanted Coco in his life. In December 1919, Boy spent several days with Chanel in Paris, before leaving for the south of France to spend Christmas with his wife. On the trip, he was in a car accident. Boy's car rolled over and burst into flames, and he died in the fire.

Coco was deeply depressed, and her emotions reached greater depths when she was prevented from attending the funeral. Instead, her friend Léon de Laborde drove her to the scene of the accident, where she stood alone and still on the scorched and blackened road. Afterward, to block out her grief, Chanel started working even harder. She promised that she would put the whole world in black for Boy.

A few months later, Coco's sister Antoinette died. After the death of their older sister, Julia, Chanel had been very protective of Antoinette. During the war, Antoinette had married a Canadian pilot and after the war she had returned to Canada with him. But before long, she ran away to Buenos Aires, Argentina. She died in Buenos Aires, far from Chanel, as a victim of the influenza epidemic that spread around the world after World War I. Once again, Coco put aside her sorrow and devoted her energy to the Chanel business.

"The Roaring Twenties"

> " Marquis Boni de Castellane did not like Chanel's designs: "Women no longer exist; all that's left are the boys created by Chanel." "

Chanel style typified the "new woman,"a woman who could work and live by her own set of rules. It was a statement the wearer made about herself. Chanel helped popularize the new feminine shape, free from clutter and corsets. Not everyone liked the new style. Some people thought the simple clothes of the new woman made her resemble a boy.

The launch of Chanel No.5

By 1920, Chanel was ready to diversify her business. In that year she met the famous Russian Grand Duke Dimitri. Thanks to Dimitri, she met Ernest Beaux, who had been employed at the Russian Czar's court. In 1921, she launched Chanel No.5. It was the first perfume to bear a **couturier's** name, and Chanel **commissioned** Ernest Beaux to make it. No.5 was the fifth formula of nine that he created for Chanel to test.

Traditionally, perfumes were blended from expensive natural ingredients, and designed to imitate flowers and other natural scents. Chanel No.5 was the first perfume blended to smell uniquely of itself rather than imitate nature. Chanel designed the simple **Modernist** bottle herself.

Coco established No.5 as the essence of the Chanel ideal. Women who might not ever be able to afford an original Chanel outfit could buy part of the Chanel style in a bottle.

To get the most sales, Chanel agreed to let Les Parfums Bourjois, France's

A design classic, Chanel's bottle for Chanel No.5 would become almost as famous as the Coca-Cola bottle.

largest perfume and make-up company, produce and market Chanel No.5. A new company was set up in 1924: Les Parfums Chanel. The agreement was that Les Parfums Bourjois would pay all of the production, marketing, and distribution costs, and Coco would receive a percentage of the profits. Such **franchising** was new in the 1920s.

Coco's relationship with Pierre and Paul Wertheimer, owners of Les Parfums Bourjois, soon became thorny. When Chanel saw what a success No.5 was, she convinced herself that she had given the rights away too cheaply and began legal proceedings to get a bigger share of the profits. By 1928, the Wertheimers had hired a lawyer whose only job was to work on Chanel's lawsuits.

Coco and the Russians

Chanel's relationship with Grand Duke Dimitri inspired many of her creations. After the 1917 **Russian Revolution,** members of the Russian **aristocracy** fled to Paris. Women who once considered embroidery a leisure activity now had to earn a living. They took jobs embroidering the large, plain blocks of fabric in Chanel's designs. Clearly influenced by her many Russian acquaintances and friends, Chanel introduced a version of the long, belted peasant blouse, made of silk, in 1922. Her embroidered dresses also became very popular.

This is an ad for Chanel's peasant blouse and embroidered dress. Coco's interest in Russia influenced both her work and her personal life.

The little black dress

By the mid–1920s, fashion was dominated by the *Garçonne* look,
which was named after a popular novel by the French author Victor
Margueritte. *Garçonnes*, called flappers in the United States, shared
Chanel's slender, almost **androgynous** figure, cropped hair, and
short hemlines. In 1926, Chanel launched her "little black dress."
Copied around the world, it became the uniform of the *Garçonne*.
The fashion designer Paul Poiret described it as "luxurious poverty."
"Simplicity does not mean poverty," Chanel replied.

The simplicity of the "little black dress" had a lasting appeal.
This 1960s Chanel original, little black dress was sold at an
auction in December 1978, for $3,000.

While men had worn black for years, women only wore it as a sign of mourning. Chanel believed black was elegant and would never go out of fashion. She hated the commotion caused by bright colors in fancy designs, like the "barbaric reds, greens, and electric blues" used by her competitors. "That can't last," she said of women in elaborate, colorful dresses. "I'm going to dress them simply, and in black."

You can have any color...

Chanel style was popular for a variety of reasons. Her straightforward designs flattered women of all different sizes, required little fabric, and were easy to copy using **mass production** techniques. **Synthetic** fibers allowed imitators to make garments at a fraction of the cost of Chanel's originals. Women who could not afford an original Chanel silk dress could easily buy a **rayon** copy.

Expensive copies came from dress shops that copied direct from the Paris fashion shows and copy houses that bought originals; less expensive copies came from manufacturers who worked from illustrations and photographs, and were therefore less exact. This range of copies flattered Chanel, who knew that no one would mistake a copy for one of her original designs.

In 1926, *Vogue* printed a picture of Chanel's little black dress. "Here is a Ford signed Chanel," the magazine announced. "The [dress] the world will wear." Comparing the dress to the Ford car, *Vogue* predicted the "little black dress" would be an essential that would make all women fashionable. Chanel was saying to women what Henry Ford said of his cars: "You can have any color, as long as it's black."

> "
> In 1927, Winston Churchill, later the prime minister of Britain, wrote to his wife after meeting Chanel: *"She hunted vigorously all day, motored to Paris after dinner, and is today engaged in passing and improving dresses on endless streams of **mannequins**. Altogether almost 200 models have to be settled in almost three weeks. Some have to be altered ten times. She does it with her own fingers."*
> "

Modern Art, Modern Style

The first three decades of the twentieth century were a time of incredible artistic development. Technological innovation, science, **mass production,** war, and political change inspired artists. Film and photography became increasingly important.

Genica Atanasiou, on the right, plays Sophocles' heroine Antigone in a cape of brown wool, one of the costumes Chanel designed for Cocteau's *Antigone*.

Chanel's association with the artistic world first began when she and Boy lived together in Paris. She had also been deeply affected by the riots at the opening night of *The Rite of Spring*. Her connections to the art world were strengthened by Misia Sert, a woman Chanel met in 1917. Misia became a lifelong friend, and Chanel later acknowledged Misia's role as her teacher in cultural and artistic subjects.

Misia introduced Coco to Jean Cocteau, an influential writer and director. In 1922,

Make it new!
Modernism, the name given to **radical** artistic experiments, encouraged both enthusiasm and violent outrage, which led to riots at *The Rite of Spring,* and fights at another ballet, called *Parade*. *Parade* was a ballet by Jean Cocteau with music that Erik Satie composed on typewriters, and outrageous costumes by Pablo Picasso. These artists were part of a group called the **avant-garde,** a name given to artists and writers whose ideas are the most modern of their time.

Cocteau asked Chanel to design costumes for his adaptation of the ancient Greek tragedy *Antigone*. Pablo Picasso, who came to dominate twentieth-century art, designed the sets, the actors' masks, and the shields.

Chanel dressed the actors in Greek-style costumes of coarse, undyed wool. Genica Atanasiou played Antigone with her hair cropped short, face whitened, and eyes rimmed in thick black make-up. Chanel dressed her in a full-length, hand-knitted coat with Greek vase motifs in maroon and black. At the last minute, feeling her contribution was being overlooked, Chanel seized a loose strand and unraveled the coat. It was too late to fix the damage, and Genica had to go on stage in one of Chanel's own coats. Another character wore a gold headband encrusted with jewels, Chanel's first effort at jewelry.

The Blue Train was inspired by the sportswear trend—a fashion Chanel had helped create.

In the reviews, Coco stole the headlines: "Chanel becomes Greek," introduced one account of the play. *Vogue* featured Chanel's costumes in February 1923.

In 1924, continuing her association with Serge Diaghilev's Ballets Russes, Chanel designed costumes for *The Blue Train*, composed by Darius Milhaud with words by Cocteau. Inspired by the fashion for sports, the ballet mixed **satire,** song, mime, and acrobatics. The name was taken from a luxury train that ran from Paris to a coastal resort town. Chanel's costumes were startling. The female lead wore a tennis outfit, and the male lead wore a golf outfit based on an outfit worn by the British Prince of Wales. One

29

dancer wore a pink bathing suit—very daring for the time—and a bathing cap that set a fashion trend.

By lending her talents to the **avant-garde,** Chanel's name became associated with **Modernism.** She was also generous in her financial support. She secretly funded a revival of Stravinsky's *The Rite of Spring* while she was involved in a relationship with the composer, and she supported Cocteau, paying his hotel bills and helping him battle his drug addiction.

Chanel designed costumes for ballets and plays throughout the 1920s. She had a flair for advertising, and she was a strong promoter of her business. In *Orphée,* Jean Cocteau's 1926 version of the ancient Greek play *Orpheus and Eurydice,* Chanel had the actresses dress in her latest fashions.

All that glistens...

The Chanel business empire took another new direction when Coco turned her love of costume jewelry into high fashion.

Costume jewelry is made from fake jewels that are designed to look real. Chanel's radical idea was to design the jewelry to match her fashions.

Costume jewelry meant women could "have fortunes that cost nothing." Chanel believed "jewels ... give an air of elegance or decoration." There was nothing more foolish than women dripping in real jewels: too much money, Chanel believed, killed luxury.

Coco, shown here in 1928, wearing strings of fake pearls, is about to get into her chauffeur-driven Rolls Royce.

As always, Chanel herself broke every convention about wearing jewelry. Traditionally women wore discreet jewelry in the daytime and more showy pieces at night. Instead, Chanel draped herself in strings of jewels during the day, even when sailing or on the beach, and in the evening often wore no jewelry at all. The fashion designer Christian Dior later said, "With a black sweater and ten rows of pearls she revolutionized the world of fashion."

Coco in love (again)

There were several men in Chanel's life after Boy, but any man who tried to force her to choose between him and her work would lose.

Coco Chanel went to the Grand National horse race in England with the Duke of Westminster in 1925.

Her most famous relationship was with the Duke of Westminster, Britain's wealthiest man. The Duke kept two yachts, and had a residence in London, a Scottish mansion, a hunting lodge in the French countryside, a suite in Paris, and a mansion in Deauville. The Duke was related to Winston Churchill, the future British prime minister.

Chanel met the Duke in Monte Carlo at Christmas 1923. Gossip magazines were soon predicting they would marry, but Chanel had no intention of sharing the Duke with other women. Once, when he tried to please her with expensive emeralds, Chanel let the emeralds slip from her hand into the ocean to show him that he could not make up for his poor treatment of her by giving her expensive things. When the relationship ended, Chanel claimed, "There have been several Duchesses of Westminster. There is only one Chanel!"

Chanel's next relationship was with Pierre Reverdy, a poverty-stricken poet. Reverdy believed happiness was an illusion. To chase pleasure, he told Chanel, was to chase the wind. His attitude was the opposite of what most people believed in the **Jazz Age,** and his poetry was unsuccessful. When he died, Chanel tried to rescue his reputation from obscurity. It was her relationship with Reverdy that inspired her to believe in an afterlife and the idea that nothing ever disappeared.

Chanel went to La Pausa, her home on the French Riviera, with her dog, Gigot, to relax.

Good Times and Bad

The House of Chanel continued to expand throughout the 1920s as it supplied the seemingly endless demand for luxury goods in Europe and the U.S. Then, in October 1929, the **New York Stock Exchange,** located on Wall Street in New York City, crashed. This event changed everything, and the **depression** that it caused dramatically hit the luxury trade.

For a while, the rich continued to amuse themselves, unconcerned by the effects that economic collapse had on their fellow countrymen and women.

The collapse of the world economy left millions of people out of work in France. Here, unemployed men line up for free soup and bread in Paris.

The Great Depression
In the years after World War I, the U.S. became the world's most powerful nation. Between 1913 and 1929, the economy grew by 70 percent. The New York Stock Exchange, on Wall Street, became the world's leading stock market. Between 1927 and 1929, share prices rose spectacularly. People used savings, borrowed, and even mortgaged homes to buy more. Then, on October 24, 1929, prices dropped suddenly. People lost businesses and homes, companies closed, and millions of people lost their jobs. Because of the importance of the U.S. to the world economy, the Wall Street Crash made economic problems around the world much worse. Foreign businesses dependent on selling things to the U.S. were hit hardest.

As late as 1930, extravagant balls were being held in Paris. However, the demand for **haute couture** soon dried up. Paul Poiret closed his fashion house and went into debt. Within months of the Wall Street Crash, 10,000 French fashion workers lost their jobs.

Gloria Swanson wore an outfit designed by Coco Chanel in the 1931 movie *Tonight or Never.*

Chanel managed to survive. Wealthy customers from India and South America made up for the loss of her American customers, and the richest of her European customers stayed loyal. In addition, by 1931 it was considered bad taste to look wealthy; rich women bought the plain dresses, plain coats, and sweaters that were the core of the Chanel line. Chanel was invited to London to promote cotton as a fashion fabric.

Coco goes to Hollywood

Sam Goldwyn, the powerful Hollywood film producer, realized that the movies had to attract more women audiences to survive the **Great Depression.** He believed women wanted movies with big stars wearing the latest clothes, and was determined to make movies with the latest fashions. This was risky—fashions could change quickly, so outfits might have been out of date by the time a film was released.

Goldwyn had first met Chanel in 1929. In 1931, she signed a contract to design outfits exclusively for his stars. Chanel, then the most famous **couturier** in the world, traveled to Hollywood, California, in a blaze of publicity. Chanel was proud of the work she did there, but her time in Hollywood was not a success. Chanel's designs turned out to be too modest for most film stars. As the *New Yorker* magazine noted on her return to France in 1932: "She made a lady look like a lady. Hollywood wants a lady to look like two ladies."

Although Chanel was forced to cut her clothes prices in half at the height of the depression in 1932, the $2 million she earned in Hollywood allowed her to keep the company going. The House of Chanel continued to expand, and it was employing over 4,000 workers by 1935.

In 1932, Chanel created a range of diamond-encrusted precious jewelry. This Chanel necklace was one of several shown at the "Diamond Jewels" exhibition in 1932.

Back to jewelry

The economic depression also offered other opportunities. In 1932, in an effort to boost sales, the International Diamond Guild **commissioned** Chanel to create a range of diamond jewelry. Chanel had belittled diamonds when she was designing costume jewelry, but she believed diamonds were a wise investment during a depression.

Working with jewelry designer Paul Iribe, Chanel presented designs based on three shapes: knots, feathers, and stars. Many pieces, extravagantly decorated with diamonds, could be used as either brooches or hair ornaments, necklaces or tiaras.

Later Chanel designed jewelry based on nature, like diamond necklaces designed to look like oak leaves and acorns. By 1939, she was sewing jeweled necklaces directly onto dresses.

Love and Politics

" Of her relationship with Paul Iribe, Chanel later said, *"He drained me, ruined my health."* "

Paul Iribe had spent the 1920s in Hollywood designing sets for the movie director Cecil B. De Mille. Returning to France, he built a successful business but lost everything in the **Great Depression.** Iribe began designing jewelry for the famous jewelry maker Cartier and for the House of Chanel. His experiences during the Depression had made him passionately **right-wing** and **anti-Semitic.**

He and Coco started a relationship in 1931, when Chanel's relationship with the Wertheimers was at a new low. Chanel No.5 had become the world's best-selling perfume, and the Wertheimers wanted to market other beauty products under Chanel's name. She opposed this, and they wanted to remove her as president of Les Parfums Chanel. She gave Iribe **power of attorney** to act for her, but he chaired a board meeting so poorly that the members voted him out. Les Parfums Chanel began granting manufacturing rights for Chanel products to other companies controlled by the Wertheimers.

As a **nationalist** and an **elitist,** Paul Iribe condemned **republican** government and wanted to see a strong ruler. He persuaded Chanel to finance his political magazine *The Witness.* It was one of many nationalistic, anti-German magazines then being published in France.

Chanel is shown here in 1931, the year she met Paul Iribe. He moved her political views to the right.

In 1934 there was an unsuccessful rebellion by right-wing militants in France. It provoked **communists** and **socialists** to form a **Popular Front.** Many people feared that **Bolshevism** was just around the corner. Influenced by Iribe, Coco moved from political indifference to a belief that socialism threatened France.

In 1934, Iribe and Chanel announced they would marry. Not everyone was happy: the novelist Colette wrote, "Iribe is marrying Chanel. Aren't you horrified—for Chanel?"

However, before they could marry, Iribe suffered a heart attack playing tennis with Chanel at La Pausa, her home in the south of France. He died in the hospital in Menton, France, at age 52. Once again, Chanel took refuge from her sorrow in her work.

Chanel and the Arts

Despite her experiences in Hollywood, Chanel had not finished with the theater, the movies, or the **avant-garde.** In 1934, she designed costumes for Jean Cocteau's *The Infernal Machine.* Cocteau was an influential artist by now, but he still relied on Chanel's support for his

Chanel's mummy-style costumes for *Oedipus the King*, by Jean Cocteau, were fiercely criticized in the press for their "indecency."

hotel bills and **detoxification** cures. When Cocteau revived the ballet *Oedipus the King*, Chanel dressed the dancers in revealing Egyptian mummy-style wrappings, which were criticized in the press as indecent.

Despite her political views, Chanel remained on good terms with many **socialist** artists. The film-maker Jean Renoir asked Chanel to create the wardrobe for his movie *The Marseillaise,* and only conflicting schedules prevented Chanel from working on his anti-war masterpiece *The Grand Illusion*. A year later, Chanel designed costumes for *The Rules of the Game*, Renoir's **satire** about a group of wealthy people

Chanel and Schiaparelli

Chanel's greatest rival was Elsa Schiaparelli, also famous for designs she created with Salvador Dali. In contrast to Chanel, Schiaparelli used vivid, even startling, colors, and was known for her use of "shocking pink." Her collections were built around colorful themes—the circus, music, and butterflies—and influences from African art. Here a model wears an outfit with butterflies on the jacket and hat.

Chanel and Schiaparelli disliked each other. Chanel called Schiaparelli "that Italian who makes clothes." Schiaparelli referred to Chanel as a "dreary little [**middle-class** woman]." But each kept a close eye on the other's work. In dividing the same pool of clients, they were creating schools of fashion: Chanel was a safe designer, and Schiaparelli was considered more adventurous.

preparing to go hunting. As they prepare to leave disagreements start, and the masters and servants turn upon and shoot each other. On opening night, the furious audience tried to set fire to Renoir's chair.

Chanel also formed a friendship with the Spanish artist Salvador Dali, a leading **Surrealist.** Dali composed *Bacchanale* for the Ballets Russes and asked Chanel to design the costumes. Later he said, "Chanel ... created some of the most luxurious costumes."

Strike at the House of Chanel

In April 1936, the people of France elected the socialist leader Léon Blum and his **Popular Front** to run the government. Blum promised to introduce paid vacation time, family support, unemployment benefits, and a 40-hour workweek.

In 1938, Chanel's love of gypsy style influenced her work. Colorful skirts were worn with embroidered blouses and short bolero jackets. Suits were decorated with bright braid and embroidery.

The French Constitution prevented Blum from taking office until June. French workers worried that the current government would prevent Blum from keeping his promises by passing laws before he took power. A wave of strikes and "sit-ins" began. Unrest spread to the textiles industry. On June 6, 1936, as Chanel arrived at work, she was confronted by a **picket line** of striking saleswomen and seamstresses who refused to let her into the House of Chanel. Seething at their behavior, Chanel retreated to her suite at the Hotel Ritz.

The wave of strikes was soon settled in return for wage increases, union recognition, a 40-hour workweek, and two weeks of paid vacation each year. Chanel responded to the settlement by firing many of the people she thought had caused the problem, but this simply made her staff more determined.

According to her lawyer, René de Chambrun, Chanel was **paternalistic.** She had little empathy with her poorly paid staff, despite growing up poor. She pretended that she did not understand the phrase **"sit-down strike,"** and claimed that workers were sitting on her dresses. However, pressure to produce a fall collection, and de Chambrun's careful advice, forced Chanel to settle.

Coco is shown here in her suite in the Ritz, in 1937. In the late 1930s, Chanel's formalwear became more elaborate.

Surviving Occupation in
World War II

Outside the world of **haute couture,** people were beginning to worry about the possibility of another war. Style and fashion seemed unimportant, and inappropriate with the threat of war. On September 2, 1939, Hitler's army invaded Poland. Britain and France declared war on Germany. Explaining that it was no time for fashion, Coco closed the House of Chanel.

The war reaches Paris

Surprisingly, after the declaration of war, a sort of peace broke out. Soldiers at the front exchanged more words than bullets; from their positions, German troops cheered soccer matches played between French infantrymen. German **propaganda** blamed England for the war. Many Frenchmen agreed, seeing little reason to die for Poland.

A blackout was put into effect in Paris, but movie theaters reopened. Fashion designers presented collections. For the rich, there were inconveniences—butlers and chauffeurs were **conscripted** and gasoline was hard to get—but otherwise, life seemed normal. Chanel took a suite at the Ritz. Jean Cocteau also stayed there, in a room Chanel paid for.

The fighting started in earnest in April 1940. Hitler's generals developed

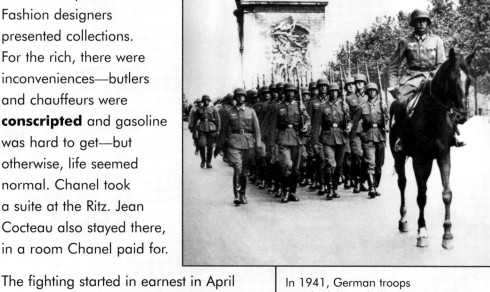

In 1941, German troops marched through the Arc de Triomphe to occupy Paris.

blitzkrieg—lightning-war. Striking suddenly, the Germans bombed and fought their way through Western Europe. On June 4, Paris was bombed and *l'exode*, the escape of the city's population, began. Millions of citizens fled, carrying what they could in buses, horse-drawn carriages, cars, bicycles, and carts.

France governed from Vichy

Chanel packed a few belongings and her collection of precious jewelry, and she and a friend set off south, away from the German forces. As they traveled, they heard the news that the Italian **Fascist** leader Mussolini had launched air raids on the south of France in support of his Nazi ally. Changing direction, Chanel and her companion traveled to Biarritz, a French town near Spain.

Meanwhile, French military leaders declared Paris an "open city" and pulled back. Within six weeks the Germans were almost at Bordeaux and the French signed a humiliating peace treaty: The Germans occupied northern France, while an "independent" French government ran the south from the town of Vichy.

In August, as the situation stabilized, Chanel decided to return to Paris. Stopping for a break in a small village, she saw a child begging. Her normal reserve cracked and she gave the child several coins. Immediately the child's mother appeared and took the money from him: "At least we will eat tonight," the woman said. This experience made Chanel aware of how most people in France were living.

French resistance

Following World War II, the French promoted an image of heroic **resistance** to the Nazi invaders. In fact, some people were willing **collaborators** in some of the Nazi's most horrible crimes. The U.S. ambassador at the time wrote, "French leaders … have accepted … becoming a province of Nazi Germany." When the Germans put **anti-Semitic** laws into place in northern France, the Vichy government went even further in its anti-Semitism.

Arriving in Paris, Chanel discovered that the Germans had taken over the Hotel Ritz, including her suite. One story claims she told the manager to inform the German officers that Chanel had arrived. Another story says a German officer noticed her luggage tag and said: "If we're talking about the Mademoiselle Chanel of fashion and perfume fame, she can stay." Whatever the truth, Chanel got a room.

Selling out

Though she had closed her **haute couture** salons in 1939, a boutique selling Chanel perfumes and accessories was still open. Coco visited it soon after her arrival in Paris. It was full of German soldiers buying Chanel No.5. When stocks ran out, the soldiers bought empty display bottles—anything to prove they had been in Paris.

Chanel's nephew, André Palasse, was being held as a prisoner of war. Chanel went to Hans Gunther von Dincklage to try to get André released. He was a former member of the German embassy staff in Paris, who was rumored to work for German military intelligence.

"My friends call me *Spatz*, German for 'sparrow,'" von Dinklage told Chanel. Despite their age difference—Spatz was twelve years younger—they lived together at the Ritz until 1944 when, as **Allied** forces were about to liberate Paris, Spatz fled back to Germany.

Under the occupation, a strange normality returned. The Germans encouraged theaters, movie theaters, and newspapers to open, and helped many of Chanel's **avant-garde** friends. Despite shortages for everyone else, luxuries were available for the German troops and the wealthy French **elite.**

Chanel had her pre-war fortune to support her, and she was still making money from the sales of Chanel No.5 throughout occupied Europe. Like many wealthy people, she and Spatz held expensive parties for the German officers and the French elite. Meanwhile, gossip magazines claimed Chanel and Cocteau were to marry. This story emerged in 1943, at a time when resistance to the invaders and the French collaborators was growing. It deflected attention from the fact that Chanel had a German companion who was a member of the occupying forces.

43

Germans stationed in France were able to enjoy the best of French culture, like this performance at a theater in Paris.

War and the Wertheimers

Around 1943, the Vichy government's Commission for Jewish Affairs took over many Jewish businesses and gave them to non-Jews. The Wertheimers, who were Jewish, had gone into hiding before escaping to the U.S., leaving their company in the hands of a cousin, Raymond Bollack. Although Chanel showed no interest in design or fashion at this time, she saw the Commission for Jewish Affairs as an opportunity to end the difficult partnership. However, Bollack found a non-Jewish industrialist to claim he ran the company and a German officer to certify everything was in order. Chanel's troubles with the Wertheimers would continue. No.5 continued to be sold by the French company and, unknown to Chanel, by the Wertheimers' smaller U.S. company.

Chanel was also involved in attempts to save Jews from concentration camps. The Jewish poet and painter Max Jacob, who was a member of the French **avant-garde,** was a friend of Chanel's. Already seriously ill, Jacob was arrested and taken to a transit camp at Drancy near Paris. The next stage of his journey would be to the death camps in Poland. Chanel helped in the desperate efforts made by his friends to save him. The authorities were eventually persuaded that he was too ill to travel, and he was released. Unfortunately, Jacob died soon after his release.

An End to Hostilities

By 1943, the United States was involved in the war in Europe and the war in the Pacific. The German army was struggling on the **Eastern Front** and facing defeat at Stalingrad in the Soviet Union and in North Africa. For many people, the question was not whether Germany would be defeated, but when and how.

Like many people, Chanel believed that the Russians would eventually defeat Germany. Hitler still believed he could defeat both the Russians and the **Allies,** but many senior Nazis thought the best option was for Germany to make a quick peace in the West, or even form an anti-communist alliance with the Allies against the Soviet Union.

There is one fascinating wartime story, the complete truth of which will never be known. During her relationship with the Duke of Westminster, Chanel met Winston Churchill, who was by now the prime minister of Britain. It was suggested that Chanel could ask Churchill to listen to secret proposals from officers in the German army, who were hoping that Germany and the Allies could arrange a peace treaty. Chanel would to go to Spain, meet the British ambassador, and request a meeting with Churchill.

The German high command agreed to this plan, and gave Chanel the go-ahead for what became known as Operation *Modellhut,* named after the German word for "hat model." Chanel asked that Vera Bate, a friend who was living in Italy, be her traveling companion. Vera was brought to Paris, where Chanel explained she needed help reopening the House of Chanel in Madrid. Vera saw the trip as an opportunity to escape occupied Europe. The involvement of German security agents in getting her from Rome to Paris made her certain that Chanel was a German spy.

When they arrived in Madrid, the women separated. Both women went to the British embassy, each certain that the other would not know where she had gone. As Chanel met with the ambassador to request a meeting with Churchill, Vera was down the hall, telling a member of the ambassador's staff that Chanel was a spy.

Operation *Modellhut* failed. Churchill was ill, and could not see Chanel, and he was firmly against compromise with Hitler's Germany. Chanel traveled back to France alone, her friendship with Vera in ruins.

Liberation and fear

After the defeat of the Germans and the liberation of France, there were scores to settle: **collaborators** were jailed, their property was seized, and women who had associated with the Germans had their heads shaved. There were many executions. Though Spatz had fled back to Germany, Chanel realized her high profile and close association with a German officer like Spatz would make her a prime target.

The journalist Malcolm Muggeridge explained how Chanel used her head to avoid being harmed during this time. Chanel placed a notice outside her perfume boutique announcing free Chanel No.5 for American soldiers. They came in huge numbers, preventing the **Free French** police from arresting her. Using this breathing space, she sought help from her contacts. Finally taken in for questioning by the Free French authorities, she was released after three hours and no charges were ever brought. It is thought that the people in power helped Chanel avoid being charged as a collaborator. They did not want Chanel to go to court, because of what she might say about their own collaboration with the Germans during the war.

Exile and fortune

The end of the war also meant the return of the Wertheimers. They had been making and selling their own Chanel No.5 in the United States, and Les Parfums Chanel was now a subsidiary of an American company, Chanel Inc. Coco realized they had made millions of dollars using her name, but her **royalties,** deposited in a Swiss bank, amounted to a few thousand dollars. She had been cheated again. To be closer to the banks and her lawyers for her lawsuit against the Wertheimers, Chanel moved to Lausanne, Switzerland.

There was another reason for her move: Spatz had been captured in Germany by U.S. troops, and he was being held as a prisoner of war. He was soon released, but a return to France was out of the question. In Switzerland, he and Chanel could live together quietly.

American soldiers lined up in front of the Chanel store in 1945 to get free No.5 perfume for their wives and girlfriends.

In 1947, Chanel and Pierre Wertheimer came to an agreement to compensate Chanel for the lost earnings. Satisfactory to both sides, the agreement renewed their business relationship. From now on, the Wertheimers and Chanel were respectful of one another's business skills and were more pleasant to each other.

Chanel was now very rich, but her name was fading from fashion consciousness. Only women with long memories remembered her style; younger women knew her only as a name on a perfume bottle. Chanel confessed she was simply a bored old woman, drifting back and forth between Switzerland and France. The war had changed her life enormously. Many of her friends died in the postwar years, and despite her move to Switzerland, her relationship with Spatz was soon over.

47

The Return of
Coco Chanel

In 1954, at the age of 71, Coco Chanel announced her comeback. The editor of *Vogue*, Bettina Ballard, said "she [returned] to escape boredom and to keep young." A woman named Marie-Hélène de Rothschild claimed credit for inspiring Chanel's return. Seeing Marie-Hélène dressed for a ball in an expensive ball gown, Chanel exclaimed "What a horror," and immediately improvised a substitute from a taffeta curtain. After the ball, Marie-Hélène reported that everyone had asked who the designer was.

In addition to the desire to design again, Chanel had financial motives. In spite of Marilyn Monroe's famous remark, "The only thing I wear in bed is Chanel No.5," perfume sales were not very strong. So Chanel moved back into the Paris Ritz, the store and the workrooms of her fashion house were renovated, and former members of staff were recruited. Coco began working on a new collection.

Chanel was photographed by Robert Doisneau on the mirrored staircase of her fashion house during her comeback in 1954.

Chanel and the New Look

Chanel still believed in the virtue of a flattering style that was easy to wear and did not go out of style quickly. But she now thought that styles that were unsuitable for most people were not fashion but fancy dress. In particular, she thought the elaborate New Look, unveiled by Christian Dior in 1947, was not the way forward. Sweeping aside practical wartime fashion, the New Look returned to luxury with long, full skirts with layers of petticoats. The New Look also emphasized tiny waists, using tight corsets to create the **hourglass** figure. One writer said these corsets pulled the waist in so much that

Dior's "New Look" exaggerated the waistline.

women had a choice between not eating or suffering painful indigestion. Chanel commented that the pulled-in waistline was "an exaggeration even on a wasp."

Chanel's 1954 collection was a response to the New Look she so despised. But it was also a response to the increasingly fashion-conscious **mass market** that demanded stylish but less expensive designs in large quantities. With this collection, Chanel would once again revolutionize fashion. By using newly available **synthetic** textiles and modern production techniques, companies could make **ready-to-wear** copies quickly and cheaply, reaching a massive audience.

Pierre Wertheimer recognized that Chanel's comeback would encourage perfume sales. He also realized that as owner of Chanel

Couture, Coco could **franchise** her name, cheapening the prestige of Les Parfums Chanel. Pierre decided he had to invest in the Chanel revival: Les Parfums Chanel paid part of the cost of the collection from their publicity budget.

In interviews, Chanel restated her philosophy: "Elegance ... means freedom to move freely." Of the Spanish designer Balenciaga she said, "Didn't his customers look like armchairs?" Coco allowed the photographer Cecil Beaton to photograph her as she worked on the new collection. This was unusual: Most designers wanted their collections to be secret until they revealed them in a fashion show.

The collection was shown to the **elite** of the fashion world on February 5, 1954. The models appeared quietly, without the spectacle of a Dior parade. The audience did not applaud the collection, and it was criticized harshly in reviews. Chanel was, commentators said, "a prisoner of the age she influenced so strongly." Other reviews were more critical: The magazine *Le Combat* ran a headline, "In the sticks with 1930 Coco Chanel." The British *Daily Express* reported, "A Fiasco—Audience Gasped!" In an interview with *France-Soir*, Coco explained: "Once, I helped liberate women. I'll do it again."

"I want to go on ... and win," she told Pierre Wertheimer. "You're right," he said, promising the support of Les Parfums Chanel. Three weeks later, the American magazine *Life* carried rave reviews. "Like her best of the thirties ... elegant dash ... easy-fitting suits that are refreshing after the 'poured-on' look." The March issue of French *Vogue* followed, with a Chanel-suited model on the cover. Karl Lagerfeld, then a young apprentice designer, said the new Chanel collection was "more intoxicating than any current fashion." Coco Chanel was back.

Coco and the men

In the years between the wars, women—Chanel, Schiaparelli, Vionnet, Grès—dominated fashion. The top names were now men: Givenchy; Mainbocher; Jacques Fath, inventor of the wasp corset; Dior; and Pierre Cardin. Schiaparelli admitted defeat and closed her fashion house in 1950.

"Dressing women is not a man's job. They dress them badly because they scorn them," said Chanel in 1953.

The men's designs were different because they worked differently. They designed on paper rather than molding their clothing on models. Designs were more daring, possibly because they did not have to wear them—practicality was secondary to effect. Outfits grew bolder and more outrageous: skirts in the shape of pumpkins and trumpets, coats like tents, and skin-tight sheath dresses. Chanel was on the side of women: clothes should be comfortable. She did not believe that designers such as Dior had women's interests at heart.

Chanel set to work on her next collection. Soon buyers and the press rediscovered Chanel: classic chic was back. She used jersey, tweeds, satin, chiffons, velvets, and **synthetic** fibers, in her favorite colors—red, black, beige, white, and blue. Women famous for their elegance wore her designs: the movie stars Grace Kelly, Lauren Bacall, Ingrid Bergman, Elizabeth Taylor, and Rita Hayworth all wore Chanel. As it does today, celebrity endorsement brought further recognition.

Chanel designed a range of clothes, including formalwear and cocktail dresses, but the Chanel Suit was her most popular design.

The Chanel Suit was copied by Saks Fifth Avenue in New York. Coco still took pleasure in imitation. With girlish glee,

This model is wearing the 1959 variation of the classic Chanel Suit.

she told of a market stand selling fake Chanels: they went, she reported, like hot cakes. "Come to my place and steal all the ideas you want," she told the press. "Fashion isn't made to be canned."

In 1957, Dior died of a heart attack and his assistant, Yves Saint Laurent, took over. His first collection paid Chanel the complement of copying her. The next two—more **radically** his own—were less well received. Chanel was sweetly cutting: "Saint Laurent has excellent taste. The more he copies me, the better taste he displays." Coco was once again the undisputed leader of fashion.

In spite of her new success, Coco was beginning to feel old and lonely. In 1955, Adrienne, the only family member she cared about, died. In 1960, Pierre Reverdy died, and in 1963, Jean Cocteau died. Chanel turned 80 in August 1963. She chose to forget her birthday.

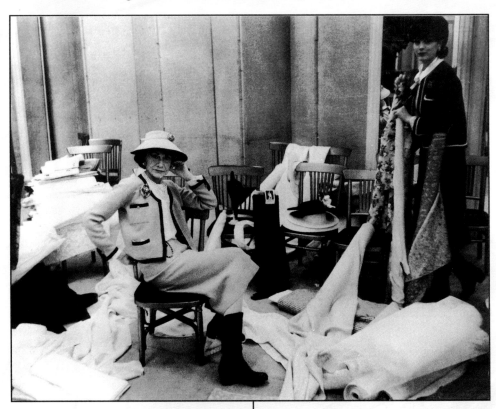

Despite projecting the image of a lady of leisure, Chanel was a tireless worker. In 1959, she was photographed at work choosing fabrics.

In the 1960s, Chanel refined her classic look. She ridiculed other designers. She ridiculed Paco Rabanne, who used aluminum and plastics in his designs, as a passing fad. She criticized Pierre Cardin for **franchising** his name and logo to every imaginable item—clothes, drinks, foods, and perfumes.

By 1968, the Chanel empire was a multimillion dollar per year business. Chanel had become a legend in her own lifetime: Coco, a musical based on Chanel's life and starring Katharine Hepburn, opened on Broadway. However, Chanel lived an increasingly lonely life. Surprisingly, when asked, she advised women to follow convention and marry instead of devoting themselves to a career. She said, "Otherwise she will need courage … and at the end she pays the terrible price of loneliness … Solitude can help a man find himself: it destroys a woman." The men she loved never understood how she felt about her work: "The House of Chanel. It was my child. I made it, out of nothing."

Chanel hated Sundays—a day empty of work. She had her chauffeur take her to Père Lachaise cemetery where she wandered among the tombs, talking to the dead, as she had done as a child. At home in the Ritz she began sleepwalking, and wandering the hotel halls. Disgusted with herself, she ordered her personal staff to lock her in at night.

In 1970, Chanel suffered a slight **stroke** that paralyzed her right arm. Many people thought that she would not survive the stroke, but they were wrong. After a lot of medical care, Coco returned to work.

On the evening of Sunday, January 10, 1971, Coco complained to her maid, Céline, that she could not breathe. Céline called the doctor, but Chanel died before he arrived. Her final words were: "You see, this is how you die."

The Mystery of Chanel

Chanel's life and opinions give us clues about her personality, but her deliberate efforts to hide the truth often covered up her true character. She was human, and thus was often contradictory. She could be cruel and crude about people—even **couturiers** who admired her. But she was also in the public eye, and everything she said or did was noted or reacted to.

There were many contradictions in her life. Although given to strong outbursts, especially on the subject of the Wertheimers, her later relationship with Pierre Wertheimer was both polite and professional. She grew up poor, but she had no sympathy for her poorly-paid staff, and viewed their protests at their small salaries as disloyal. Chanel devoted herself to her career and never married, but she encouraged other women to marry rather than having careers.

This 1937 classic portrait of Chanel, by Horst P. Horst, established Horst's reputation as a photographer. He was always grateful to Chanel for it.

The legacy of Chanel

Cecil Beaton wrote, "Chanel had … Talents that are very rare, she was a genius, and all her faults must be forgiven for that reason."

In 2000, *Time* magazine identified Coco Chanel as one of 100 people who changed the twentieth century. Women.com named her as one of their "100 Women of the

Millennium." Today, the House of Chanel is a **multinational** fashion and perfume empire. In 1983, the designer Karl Lagerfeld produced his first collection for the House of Chanel. He is still the head fashion designer, and he incorporates many of Coco Chanel's classic innovations into his own designs. It has been estimated that the Chanel group brings in more than $2 billion each year.

Ultimately, however, Coco Chanel will be remembered as an artist, an **iconoclast,** a revolutionary, and as a feminist. As Jean Cocteau observed, she brought to fashion the eye and techniques of the artist. She ridiculed **belle époque** fashions and realized women's changing roles demanded new styles. After World War I, women's status would never be the same, and Chanel was ready with clothes that suited their growing independence. As the first "star designer," she broke through rigid class barriers and joined a world of wealth and privilege. She explained, "One did not talk to tradespeople when I started. One did not recognize them if one ran into them at the races and one certainly didn't invite them to dinner."

Chanel not only revolutionized fashion itself, but also the business of fashion, and she had a major influence on generations of designers. She was at the center of a **revolution** in art and culture, an intimate friend of the leading lights of the **avant-garde,** and witness to and participant in some of the most notable artistic events of the twentieth century.

Although she denied she was a feminist, Coco Chanel lived as one. She disregarded what society deemed proper for women and earned success as a businesswoman at a time when few women had such confidence or such opportunities. She lived by her own rules, and would not be intimidated into compromising them. She designed clothes for the new, assertive woman. And she lived her life as an assertive and confident woman.

> " Artist, writer, and film-maker Jean Cocteau said, *"Chanel has, by a kind of miracle, worked in fashion according to rules that would seem to have value only for painters, musicians, poets."* "

Timeline

1883	Chanel is born on August 19, in Saumur, France.
1895	Chanel's mother, Jeanne, dies. Chanel and her two sisters are sent to an orphanage in Aubazine, France.
1900–02	Chanel and her sister Julia attend boarding school at Moulins.
1900–04	Chanel works as a dressmaker with her aunt, Adrienne, performs as a singer in Moulins and earns the nickname "Coco," and meets Etienne Balsan.
1905	Chanel moves to Royallieu with Etienne Balsan.
1908	Chanel meets Arthur "Boy" Capel while on vacation with Balsan in the French Pyrenees.
1909	Chanel opens her first **millinery** business in Paris.
1910	With the support of Boy Capel, Chanel opens a new store in Paris.
1912	The actress Gabrielle Dorziat is photographed wearing a range of Chanel hats.
1913	Encouraged by Boy, Chanel opens a fashion house in Deauville, France, a fashionable resort town. Chanel's sister Julia dies.
1914	World War I begins.
1915	Chanel opens a fashion house in Biarritz.
1916	Chanel pioneers the use of jersey material as a fashion fabric.
1918	World War I ends.
1919	Chanel is praised as one of the artists of the **avant-garde.** Boy Capel dies in a car accident.
1920	Chanel meets Russian Grand Duke Dimitri in Biarritz. Chanel introduces the first Chanel Suit and the cloche hat.
1921	Chanel launches Chanel No.5 and designs the Minimalist bottle. Chanel opens a fashion house in Paris.
1922	Chanel designs the costumes for Jean Cocteau's adaptation of *Antigone*, and introduces the *Roubachka*, an embroidered Russian peasant blouse.
1923	To increase the sales of Chanel No.5, Chanel signs a manufacturing and distribution agreement with the owners of Les Parfums Bourjois, Pierre and Paul Wertheimer. Chanel meets the Duke of Westminster.

1924	Chanel creates Les Parfums Chanel in partnership with the Wertheimers.
	Chanel designs ballet costumes for *The Blue Train*.
	Chanel begins a relationship with the Duke of Westminster.
	Chanel starts to design costume jewelry.
1926	Chanel launches the groundbreaking "little black dress."
1929	The effects of the Wall Street Crash and the **Great Depression** hit the French fashion industry.
1930s	Chanel designs and refines a range of evening gowns and suits, and continues to design costumes for the theater, movies, and ballet.
1931	Chanel is hired by MGM to work in Hollywood, where she designs costumes for *Tonight or Never*.
	Chanel begins a relationship with Paul Iribe.
1932	Chanel returns to Paris and is commissioned to design a range of diamond jewelry.
1934	Chanel announces her engagement to Paul Iribe; he dies of a heart attack before they can marry.
1939	World War II begins, and Chanel closes her **haute couture** salons.
1940	Chanel flees to Biarritz, France, and then returns to Paris. She settles in the Hotel Ritz.
	Chanel meets Hans Gunther von Dincklage, called "Spatz," and they begin a relationship.
1943	Chanel plans to meet Winston Churchill in what becomes known as Operation *Modellhut*.
1945	World War II ends.
	Chanel leaves Paris for Lausanne, Switzerland.
1954	Chanel stages a comeback at age 71: the range includes suits, overcoats, cocktail dresses, formalwear, and costume jewelry.
1968	Coco, a Broadway musical based on Chanel's life, opens in New York City.
1971	Chanel dies at the Hotel Ritz, Paris, on January 10, aged 87.

Glossary

affluent society name given to the wealthy postwar world of the 1950s

Allies refers to the countries that fought against Germany in World War II, including the UK, the Soviet Union, France, and the U.S.

androgynous having both male and female characteristics, used to describe boyish fashion

anti-Semitism anti-Jewish feelings and actions

aristocracy group of people who are members of the class that rules a country and inherit their wealth and position from their parents

avant-garde pioneers or innovators in the arts

belle époque period in France that lasted from 1900 until the start of World War I

Bolshevism violent, revolutionary form of communism that took over in the Soviet Union after the Russian Revolution

Claudines female characters in the works of the novelist Colette, and women who imitated the style and lifestyle of those characters

collaborator someone who assists or cooperates with invaders

commission to hire someone to create something for you

communist believer in a political idea that has at its heart the idea of equality for all, and ownership of all property; associated with Karl Marx and the 1917 revolution in Russia

conscript to demand that someone enters the army

couturier person who designs, makes, or sells fashionable clothes

depression period of serious economic crisis, featuring high unemployment, falling prices, and rising numbers of company closures

detoxification process undergone by alcoholics and drug-addicts to clear their bodies of drugs and help them defeat addiction

dowry money that a woman brings into a marriage; a large dowry would allow a woman to marry into another wealthy family

Eastern Front scene of conflict between the German and Russian armies

elite rich upper classes, a superior or select few

elitist person who believes that a select group of people is better than other groups

etiquette social manners and rules of correct behavior

exile being forced to leave a country and live elsewhere, usually because of political beliefs

fascist supporter of Fascism, a form of extreme dictatorship, characterized by aggressive nationalism and anti-communism

fertility ability to get pregnant and have children

franchise permission given by a company for a retailer to sell its goods

Free French French government-in-exile led by Charles de Gaulle during World War II

garrison town town where lots of soldiers are based

Great Depression economic slump that followed the Wall Street Stock Market crash of 1929, when businesses failed and unemployment rose dramatically

haute couture high-class dressmaking

hospice hostel for homeless or poor families and individuals; often supported by church funds, charities, or town councils

hourglass exaggerated female shape with a tiny waist, achieved by using tight corsets

iconoclast person who attacks the beliefs that many people hold dear

illegitimate born out of wedlock

illiterate unable to read and write

industrialization growth of industry, mass production, and the factory system

inferiority complex belief a person has that makes him or her feel he or she is less important, intelligent, or worthy than other people

Jazz Age period of wealth, freedom, and spending between the end of World War I and the beginning of the Great Depression in 1929; sometimes called the Roaring Twenties

mannequin person who models clothing while standing still

mass market large-scale consumer market for products, and the development of manufacturing techniques capable of satisfying the market

mass production making things in large numbers using factory and production-line techniques

middle class group of people between the aristocracy and the poor

milliner hat-maker

Modernism name given to the art movement of the early twentieth century, characterized by the use of unusual and unconventional subjects and techniques

multinational large company that is not based in a single country but is divided between several countries, and has a worldwide market for the goods it produces

nationalist putting the interest of one nation and national group above all else, and turning against outsiders, foreigners, foreign powers, and religious minorities

New York Stock Exchange center for the buying and selling of shares in companies, located on Wall Street in New York City

pagan fertility rite ceremony associated with pre-Christian religion, that is performed to make the land grow crops

parasol umbrella that protects people from the sun

paternalistic limiting people's freedom by imposing well-meaning but strict regulations

picket line line of workers outside a workplace who are trying to make people aware that their workplace does not treat them fairly

Popular Front alliance of communists and socialists that won the 1936 elections in France

power of attorney delegated authority; legal permission to act on another's behalf

propaganda biased broadcasts and news stories

radical term describing intense and far-reaching political, social, cultural, and artistic change

rationing system imposed during war that gives a certain amount of food, fuel, and other necessities to each person in a country

rayon a silk-like man-made fabric that is cheaper than silk

ready-to-wear ready-made fashions bought off the rack

republican person who believes in a system of government with an elected head of state and without a royal family

resistance organized opposition to invaders

revolution extreme and rapid change brought about by single-minded, violent, or confrontational means

right-wing having conservative political views, being opposed to socialism and communism

royalty payment made to a designer, artist, or author for selling copies of his or her work

Russian Revolution takeover of power by the communists in Russia in 1917 that ended the rule of the Russian royal family

satire comedy that pokes fun at popular beliefs or opinions

sit-down strike when workers come to their place of work but refuse to either work or go home

socialist person who believes in a more equal distribution of wealth and goods

stroke when an artery in the brain is blocked or breaks under pressure, and a person loses consciousness, feeling, and the ability to control his or her body

suffrage right to vote in a society. Universal suffrage is the right of all citizens, regardless of gender, creed, religion, income, race, or class to vote in elections.

Surrealist participant in the artistic movement called Surrealism

synthetic artificial, man-made

women's rights demand for women to have the right to vote, the right to work, and the right for equal treatment before the law

Places to Visit

These museums have departments on the history of textiles, fashion, and costume. Some have displays that feature outfits and pieces of jewelry by Chanel, and all of them are good places to learn about textiles and fashion.

Brooklyn Museum of Art
Costumes and Textiles Department
200 Eastern Parkway
Brooklyn, N.Y. 11238
718-638-5000

Cooper-Hewitt National Design Museum
Textile Collection
91st Street and 5th Avenue
New York, N.Y. 10028
212-849-8400

Los Angeles County Museum of Art
Costumes and Textiles Department
5905 Wilshire Blvd.
Los Angeles, Calif. 90036
323-857-6000

The Museum for Textiles
55 Centre Ave.
Toronto, Ontario M56 2H5
Canada
416-599-5321

Texas Fashion Collection
University of North Texas
Denton, Tex. 76203
940-565-2732

More Books to Read

Baker, Patricia. *Fashions of a Decade: The 1940s.* New York: Facts on File, 1991.

Baker, Patricia. *Fashions of a Decade: The 1950s.* New York: Facts on File, 1992.

Baker, Wendy, and Diane James. *Fashion.* Chicago: World Book Inc., 1997.

Black, Judy. *Fashion.* Parsippany, N.J.: Silver Burdett Press, 1994.

Costantino, Maria. *Fashions of a Decade: The 1930s.* New York: Facts on File, 1992.

Giocobello, John. *Careers in the Fashion Industry.* New York: Rosen Publishing Co., 2000.

Herald, Jacqueline. *Fashions of a Decade: The 1920s.* New York: Facts on File, 1991.

Hodgman, Ann. *A Day in the Life of a Fashion Designer.* Mahwah, N.J.: Troll Communications, 1997.

Watson, Linda. *Fashions 1900–1949.* Broomall, Pa.: Chelsea House Publishers, 2000.

Watson, Linda. *Fashions 1950–2000.* Broomall, Pa.: Chelsea House Publishers, 2000.

Index